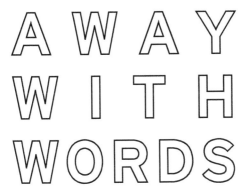

AWAY WITH WORDS

TAYLOR L. CIAMBRA

ISBN: 978-1-7370498-0-7
EPUB ISBN: 978-1-7370498-1-4
First edition published April 2021.

Cover, interior, and EPUB design by Megan Crayne
Published by CRAYNE BOOKS | craynebooks.com

Printed & distributed through IngramSpark

Fonts Soleil and Interstate licenses by Adobe Fonts

AWAY WITH WORDS

TAYLOR L. CIAMBRA

CRAYNE BOOKS
New York City, NY

CONTENTS

For
M.

WHEN I WAS YOUR AGE

but if this works,
we'll have the best
"When I was your age"
stories to tell

When I was your age,
loving each other was
the scariest thing we did,
which is why it
helped that we were
best friends first

When I was your age,
we sat on airplanes for hours
and video chatted for days.
theirs was the first text
I woke up to
and the last I read
before falling asleep

When I was your age,
"dates" and "errands"
were very often
the same thing
because we didn't
have a lot of time
or a lot of money

When I was your age,
we chose to stay
together
in a world that was
breaking up

but if it didn't work,
what stories would we
have to tell?

IT WAS CRISP

it was crisp

the feeling of
the leather jacket
on my shoulders
and the cool breeze
of September on my neck
a motorcycle rumbled by
as I walked across
my churched town,
to the black box theatre
alone and in love
with independence

it was crisp

LOVING ME IS KIND OF LIKE
BORROWING A LIBRARY BOOK

when I say that loving me
is kind of like borrowing a library book

I mean that I'll never belong to you
my pages come dog-eared
and coffee-stained
my words are highlighted
and underlined
in the margins,
you'll see thoughts penciled in
messy cursive and neat script
I've already been somebody's favorite

check me out

but don't expect to feel like
we've had enough time together
I have a return date
and a hold list

MY LAST NAME

my last name really sounds
like the sea pulling at the sand
before rushing back again
it came from sunshine but
it doesn't have tan lines
while it has the endurance to travel,
it likes to stay put wherever it finds
la dolce vita

my last name will
lay across your kitchen table,
eager to feed you
with words and food and attention
it tastes like the perfect pizza crust-
thin and chewy and salty
warm against your lips
it will get you drunk on laughter
and embrace you
with all of those open-mouthed
vowel sounds

yes, my last name is flirting with you
it has been wondering about you all night
because it wants to know if your last name
sinks into espresso and sugar like it does

Y = MX + B

I studied her the way
I should have studied the algebra
in my textbook
if I was solving for Y
she was B

          "Boyfriend" because of her height
          "Bitch" because of her opinions
          "Beautiful" because of her looks
          "Brilliant" because of her brains

but I didn't understand the first half
of the equation
and that MX was me

FALLING IN LOVE WITH OURSELVES

it was a long,
dark sleep
no dreaming,
no interruptions
till morning

your heartbeat
pulsing beside my head
was mine echoing next to yours?

another night falling asleep
beside the distance
and falling in love with ourselves

TIME WAS IRRELEVANT

time was irrelevant
wherever the sun was,
whatever phase the moon was in,
didn't matter
we were awake and alive,
          (even if it was just barely)
and that was enough
to get up and go
never minding the clocks
on our way out the door

DRIVING FOR THIS LONG

that's the thing about driving for this long
whatever happened earlier in the day
feels just as close no matter
how far away you get
and whatever's up ahead
feels just as far away
no matter how close you get

SOME PEOPLE WOULD SAY

"Some people would say
We are dating,"

you said
making us both
uncomfortable

you laid out the evidence:
the amount of time we spent together,
the errands we ran,
the doctor's appointments
we drove to,
the work events you were
my plus one at,
the pedicures on Sundays,
the hikes,
the out of state travel,
the sleepovers,
the midnight makeouts,
and the housesitting sex

I knew what it looked like
and I knew what it sounded like
but it felt different
than what either of those conclusions
would lead someone to believe

We loved each other
but we weren't in love
We were dating
but we didn't want the label
We were committed
but not exclusive

whatever it was,
it was perfect for me
in its ambiguity

IT WAS THE HOTTEST DAY OF THE YEAR

it was the hottest day of the year
and I was never going to be
cool enough to avoid one last
backward glance at you

strapping on your helmet,
and pedaling off to the river
you left me with ease

squinting against the
glare on my glasses
I wondered

       what we meant to each other

PROVOCATIVE GRAPEFRUIT

it was an early winter morning;
dark and cold and tired
I rubbed the porous rind
between my hands
considering
it's seasonal sweetness

the teeth of the spoon
bit down hard
revealing
the tart, pink aliveness
of the fruit's flesh

kissing him
could be like this
I thought
with a shiver

CAPE COD DOESN'T DISAPPOINT

we were renting time
before my boyfriend came back and
before your girlfriend did too
I remember it as one long afternoon
where I held my ear up to your chest
and tried to hear the ocean that swirled there

when you kissed me
for the first time
I tasted saltwater

A HEART-SHAPED DATE CAKE

a heart-shaped date cake
lingers in winter sunlight
toffee scent wafting

CHICKEN AND WAFFLES

I ordered the chicken and waffles
because I wanted to try out
the crunch and the sweetness
gravy pooling with the
maple syrup into pockets

I ate the chicken first,
then the waffles
much to your chagrin

"You're supposed to
eat them together,
that's the point"
you told me

I advocated for
the gravy and the syrup
they tied the flavors together
they were the *idea* of the meal
savory and sweet
breakfast and lunch

We were tired and teasing each other
but I know what you almost said
and that you almost meant it

which probably should have been
as comforting
as breakfast for dinner

much to my chagrin
I thought I could keep us
separate
like with the chicken
and with the waffles
enjoying the idea
of our combination

REUNION

the day he arrives, I will have pockets of forgetful-
ness. between laundry and dishes and text mes-
sages, I will forget he's coming.

the two hours before, I will remember. I will
thoughtlessly empty files from my laptop. the
ones I haven't used since college. the satisfying
cyber crinkle sounds as I empty the trash.

the half-hour before, my coat is on and I'm pacing
my room. waiting for a text that will not come if the
bus is running on time.

twenty minutes before, I'm in the car.

five minutes before, it's the bus station bathroom.
I don't have to pee and I'm not going to throw up,
but my body always thinks I need to.

three minutes before, I'll be on a bench near the
station doorway pretending to read or looking at
my phone or my hands. thinking everything and
nothing. hopeful and fearful.

the moment before. I see him or he sees me. if
he sees me, he'll look at me with some vague and
tired sense of expectation and amusement before
I look up and catch anything else. if I see him,

his eyes are always forward, green and blue and blank. swaggering behind a group of miserable looking people. I like him best when he's at a distance like this. I am so used to seeing him close up or in my imagination.

then my hands will twist his bag around my fingers, blood pulsing fast under the pressure. I'll say something kind and stuttered and stupid because my brain and my mouth can't coordinate in moments like these. and what is there to really say? he'll kiss me and I won't think about the cop in the corner or if we're stopping the flow of people exiting the bus. I will start to taste him when he pulls away to say, "hi."

the day I arrive, I will have pockets of forgetfulness. Between laundry and dishes and text messages, I will forget where I'm going.

before dinner, I will remember. I will load up my fork with hot bites of chicken pot pie and burn the roof of my mouth. I will take from the fridge and counter all the food I want to bring because he doesn't have much in the way of groceries. I run into my room to double-check my backpack, finally placing my phone charger and laptop into its stuffed belly.

the half-hour before, my coat is on and I'm pacing my room, asking myself if I have everything.

twenty minutes before, I'm in the car, shuttling into the shadowy night of New Haven.

five minutes before, it's the bathroom. I don't have to pee and I'm not going to throw up, but my body always thinks I need to.

three minutes before, I'm waiting in the hallway near where the bus parks. There's a line forming and I nod and smile amicably when someone asks me if this bus is going to New York City. I look at my ticket and double-check the date and time. then my phone for the date and time.

the driver opens the door out into the cold night. standing beside the big bus, they check my ticket. I stow away my backpack in a corner that I hope is easy to get to again by the time I get to port authority. I find a window seat with a charger, somewhere in between the front of the bus and the back of the bus. I plug in my phone and head-phones, pull up spotify, and hope no one sits next to me. they usually don't. I text him that I'm on my way and then get lost in the music and the traffic for two hours.

in the fluorescent light of the bus station, I wrench my too-heavy backpack from the bowels of the bus. pulling it onto my back in victory, I shuffle bleary-eyed to the subway. with a crinkled twenty, I reload my metrocard and get on a brooklyn bound train on the ACE line. I slide easily into a blue plastic seat and reciprocate frowns to my meager companions. 14th street never comes fast enough, despite the train's screeching halt and blurred alterations of light and darkness. the L train comes fast, but I sit on a sticky wooden bench because my back hurts. I double-check the subway map. the air is thick in the way that only it can be when it's underground and manufactured. a robotic voice calls, and my heart leaps. I remember that I have been meaning to give that voice a name, but still, I don't. the L train is arriving and my mind goes blank with anticipation. I count down the stops before morgan ave after each stop we make. it's always one less but I count all of the stops anyway so it's 1, 2, 3, 4, 5 and then 1, 2, 3, 4. there's no one to push past as the doors open with a suctioned pop. pushing through the turnstile, and clambering to the street above, I start to lose my breath.

the night is cold and the street is empty. it's always brighter than I remember. people are always so scared of cities at night, but white light floods out from lamp posts so much so that I don't even have a shadow. reaching the corner of the block, to my left I take in the glimmering city and to my right, a yellow submarine glows. that's the way. I jog under the weight of my backpack, past the submarine sign for the thrift store and the garage doors with graffiti. when popeye's comes into view, I know it's time to cross the street. the "shops at the loom" window is dark and my fingers click away on a keypad that's slick with more germs than I care to think about. I'm buzzed up and then there are four flights of stairs before a locked door. at this divide, we meet. bubbling with sweat and tiredness, rambling with the momentum of the subway, he'll kiss me and twist a bag out of my hand. lacing together our free palms and fingers, we'll brave the labyrinth of the fourth-floor hallways, making our way to apartment #409.

FLUSHING AVE

there is cat hair felted into the bathmat
and empty beer cans hiding under
the coffee-kitchen table

in the shadow of the neighboring building
the living room turns into a cave,
high ceilinged and dark
the walls perspire and echo
with the neighbor's cooking and lovemaking

I tell you over in the kitchen that

      I don't live here

and you say that you know,
that you're not asking me to

      live.   here.

my feet stick to the floor

I try to forget the bathmat
and work on the dishes

AFIKOMEN

I would have found it sooner
if I hadn't wanted to keep
everything exactly the way you left it

your winter coat hangs
expectantly by the front door,
above your boxy leather shoes
which stand neatly beside my hiking boots

balled up between the bedsheets
your dress socks
cuddle up next to me at night

and your razor and toothbrush
laze about in the bathroom drawer

thinking I had found
all of the things you left behind
I cleaned the kitchen mournfully
breadcrumbs were the only trace of you there
and because of the ants they had to go
except right on top of the microwave,

under a bright orange napkin
you had hidden the afikomen
my last little piece of you

IN LIGHT OF THE PAST FOUR MONTHS

purple string lights hang
like a canopy above your bed
curled up against me
like a little spoon
in a crowded drawer
you ask me if I thought
it would be this hard
I tell you yes
my brain had
crunched the numbers,
knew the logic of these things
but my heart didn't know yet
just beating into me,

      try try try

in the glow of
spindly Hanukkah candles
we hold each other
day five and almost month four
of celebrating
ordinary miracles
there is something ancient
buried into us
and something so new,
so just born about us
burning with all
who have come before

we remember our part
of this tradition

a moonless blackout of a night
finds us melting into each other
a kind of holding and becoming
asking if we can feel how much
we mean to the other
in light of the past four months

HEAD AGAINST HEART

we should live together

your head against my heart

asked where?

THE BEST COAST

with you,

I sleep on toasted marshmallows
and am full of bottom shelf ideas
that set us giggling in rain clouds
it's not always pizza and pambiche though
there are liquid sunshine days
and leaky shit buckets

but between you, me, and the sea
the best coast
is the one

        we're both on

BEING THE BOYFRIEND

your fingers loosen the tension tight
plait of muscle in my back
after all these days
of standing rigidly in three-inch heels
and smiling with the perfectly
lipsticked mouth of

     The Girlfriend

for your parents and friends
my legs unlock
like the clasp on a pearl necklace
unrestricted by pencil skirts
and polite society
they lie open and wide;
taking up space on our bed
the formality of a bra
tossed somewhere
on the midnight floor
your half-moon shape
snuggles against my chest
and my leg hair tickles your toes
I squeeze you tight enough
for us both to ache

sometimes,
I get to be

     The Boyfriend

WE PLANTED HERE

between the morning's sleepy fog
and the afternoon's relaxed sunlight
the sunflowers are just turning
their seedy faces to the road
golden petals stretch out to say

      hello and goodbye

like the Beatles song
you sang in the van
making me fall in love with you
all over again
the almanac didn't call
for all the rain we've had
and we both predicted it
would have been warmer

so many plots and plans were made
and unmade this season
few tomatoes grew and
I forgot all about the peas
but in the shadow of the year
the roots hold fast to the soil

      I am glad we planted here

IT'S OKAY TO CRY FOR LOVE

Domenico's kitchen was a home
for my inherited memories

the hot pizza was laid out
for us in welcome
I thought of Michele and Luisa,
the great grandparents I spent
all week looking for
how they must have stared down the ocean
eating their last pizza at home,
just as we are

> did they love like we do,
> irrationally and earnestly?

> did they fear like we do,
> logically and deeply?

I brought the perfect slice to my lips
the prosciutto shone under the grated parmesan
and the sauce was familiar and bright

> but it was the basil that got me

the smell a synonym for

> "share this moment"

it brought tears to my eyes and
your head to my shoulder

va bene piangere per amore

BATHROBE SEASON

I woke up to you reminding me
that it is autumn
the very word chilling my nose
and kissing my lips with nutmeg

it would be the first day of
legitimately wearing my flannel bathrobe
and drinking hot cider in the mornings

it was steadying,
the season changing
I thought as I
zipped up my jeans and
folded over my turtleneck

SUNDAY MORNING AT
DOMINIQUE ANSEL

We woke up at six-thirty.

you grumbled good-naturedly on the subway and I talked too much about this month's cronut flavor. a flavor you weren't going to like but would order one so I could have two for the price of one. you went because you wanted to spend time with me.

It's March.

We're standing in line and it's cold. cold enough for my glasses to fog up when you lean in to kiss me. my arm looped through yours, my fingers wearing your gloves, I think about our birthdays.

You'll be twenty-four. I'll be twenty-five.

people tell us we're kids still but I think about how much more we were kids when we first met. I look at the women in front of us who are probably our age or maybe even a little older. but it's j. crew catalog older. flawlessly older. how you look when you live in the east village older.

it makes me feel one hundred years old. like waiting in line for cronuts is what we do instead of going to fellowship hour after church. understanding this feels alright. seeing a silver hair on the back of your head as you open the door to the bakery, feels alright too.

DEATH OR DEBT OR DREAMS

We weren't scared of
death or debt or dreams

When we were sixteen
and jumping on your trampoline

        now-
in the uncertainty of adulthood,
we aren't free to ignore reality

I don't know if I'm right
or if I'm scared
but I know I'm right to be scared

BAGGAGE

weighing my bag in her hands
she asks if "this is all"
I brought
unable to feel the weight
carried in my heart

THE RAIN

the rain
is the steadiest thing
about this life

you hung up lavender
so we could breathe
in dreams
the covers
cool and cotton
enveloped us

waiting

my skin was burned and peeling
you pressed against it
a tight knot
another question
I was holding on to

waiting

the clouds frothed
each shade of grey
deeper than the last
thunder rumbled like
an upstairs conversation

waiting

a kiss

the rain
is the steadiest thing
about this life

UNMAKING THE BED

every night feels a little like
sunday morning now

unmaking the bed to slide into sheets
the color of cool campfires
and as soft as old college t-shirts
I pull over the quilt
white and puffy and crinkled
like a cloud you'd see elephants in
when all of life was looking up

white was a mistake, you thought
kissing the sweetness
from my strawberry jam hands
and snuggling closer to the dream

MAKING BREAKFAST FOR YOU

it was an old way,
the oldest way I knew

it was waking up early
and not touching my hair
it was wrapping a flannel bathrobe
around my tired pajamas
and finding every cool ingredient
in the bright refrigerator

there were eggs to scramble
tomatoes to slice
onions to dice
and cheese to sprinkle

it was an old way,
the oldest way I knew
to say I love you

from bed
you talked to me
about the weather
we reviewed today's plans
and recreated yesterday's laughter

it was an old way,
the oldest way you knew
to let me
tell you

IT NEEDS TO BE SAID

the knuckles of my toes
had just nestled into the arch
of your foot
and your arm had found
the best way
to lay across my shoulder
eyes half open
your quietest voice spoke:

    "I'll miss you"

it was too obvious and too painful
to say over and over again
as true as it always was
so we tried not to

but now
it feels like it needs to be said
and it needs to be heard

COME WHATEVER MAY

in the loneliness of airport terminals
and cramping up in my crooked spine
was the knowing that I was leaving
an ancient love

      for another, wilder one

I could still feel
the burn of your beard above my lips
and scrambled to pinpoint

      the exact moment when

your body heat had leached from my skin
I memorized the unreadable look in your eyes
as they peered over the loft's edge
and how the cat wrapped himself up by your head
in the glow of the night-morning light

all the while the sun rose
and seatbelts were fastened
to the hum of the airplane's
determined engine
the city's jagged smile
flashed me one last goodbye
before I was slingshot

      clear across the country

my heart stretched and strained
hammering hard enough to break
but with your words, it wouldn't

your thoughts on paper
had mirrored my own
becoming a blue-lined map
of the previous year
a perfectly penned poem
to parts sort of known
promising to love

come whatever may

TRUE ENOUGH LOVE

I was alone on the mountain

shivering against the dying coals
and the memory of when
we shared a sleeping bag
if the only thing that got me

up and down

that rocky, untraveled road
that steep tangle of trees
was thinking of you,
returning to you,

then it was true enough love

AS GOOD AS OUR WORDS

are we as good as our words?

they are the only things that
bridge the distance between us
and sometimes I wonder

if I am who
I say I am

but when my words
come back to me
through you

I know that I am
and that we are

PERHAPS THIS POEM WILL WORK

I have laid out breadcrumbs
and turned on the porch light
I sit in the doorway
and wait out the night
I turn away men with their
hearts in their hands
I blink away sleep
and fold up old plans
hoping that one day
you'll walk through the door
and feel at home
on these worn-out floors

THINK ABOUT IT

"So you've thought about it?"

Of course, I've thought about it.
That's all that lonely people do.

Think about it.

WHAT I DON'T WANT TO BE

I don't want to be anybody's

      girlfriend or boyfriend

not even yours
it's nothing against you or them

      I'm just exhausted

I don't want to coordinate schedules
or care about your feelings

      and I don't want to be the reason

somebody goes to therapy
I just want to get high on the front porch,
watch the light play in the trees,
and breathe in the mild winter

GRIEVING THE FOURTH PLACE

I looked into my life,
not its past, present, or future
but some adjacent fourth place

when grief's cold hands
reached out to touch my eyes
with tears and with shadows
silently asking for rest

LEARNING A LESSON

women kept telling me that
he learned a lesson on me
as if I cared about his development
while I lived my life
feeling tired and angry and empty

I am not some classroom
for men to make all their mistakes in
I am not a teacher who agreed
to instruct them on
how to talk to me,
touch me,
love me

what had I ever learned from men in return
except how to be fearful and insecure
how to shoulder disappointment

RUB SOME DIRT ON IT

she warned me,

> "don't put a bandaid on
> what needs stitches"

but I could do worse
than that
I thought,
lying next to you

this could be like spitting
and rubbing dirt on it

KNITTED TOGETHER

alone on the train platform
the wind nipped at my neck
like you used to

I thought of the scarf
you knitted last Christmas

evergreen and just a little too short
boxed up in my attic now
while I shivered

MISSING YOU

my weight rolls
into the soles of my feet
and digs into my heels

      just the way that yours does

my eyes close when I smile
in that sleepy, yet gleeful way
and only in the very early morning

      just the way that yours does

my head lolls back
with confidence in conversation
around new people

      just the way that yours does

my lips smirk
every now and then
for some secret reason

      just the way that yours does

missing you
has meant

      becoming you

this aloneness
feels so together

RUNNING LATE

I didn't like the idea of
being on a break
any more than you did
but we also didn't like the idea of
being apart forever

it wasn't something we could
hold each other
accountable to
at least you said you wouldn't
and I knew I shouldn't
but it got me out of the fog
and into the moment

at least for now
thinking that
my wife is out there
somewhere
he's just running

       a little late

PEOPLE WANTED TO KNOW

people wanted to know
if I had been through this before
if I knew when to eat ice cream
and how to sweat it out

what drugs to do and
which type of people to sleep with

how exactly would I keep busy?
did I know some memories would fade?
and others would become a yardstick
I measured everyone else against?

did I know that eventually,
I would be okay?

MONDAY BRUNCH

we found a Monday
brunch place
and were waiting
on the french toast

I adjusted my jacket
and took notes
on us and California
that day
I couldn't get enough
of that sun
on my face

"I feel like Fitzgerald."
I said to you,
feeling the alcohol
and remembering my Zelda
the one I was in love with,
the one who was arguably
ruining my life
but bettering my writing

you looked at me
with your sunglasses
and lit cigarette,
agreeing

      "me too,
      totally."

THERE WERE ONLY THREE THINGS

there were only three things
I knew I wanted
after you:

      sunshine,

      sweetness,

      and rest

I KNOW I DON'T SAY THIS ENOUGH

I know I don't say this enough,
but I love you

I love how you slide your fingers
between your toes and
say "thank you" during yoga

how curious you are, about everything
and especially how your laugh sounds
when you're laughing at me
you take such good care of us
even when my pride tries to stop you

I know I don't say this enough either,
but I am sorry

I don't always see
the good that you do,
when you do it
I doubt you when I know
you're already doing
what you think is best,
what you think is right

when I already know how
careful and thoughtful you are
how hard these decisions are and
how tired and scared you are

when I put that ring on your finger
every morning
I remember how we
promised each other the world
and I see that you are giving it to us

it's difficult to find
the right words to contain
who we are and
how I feel about us
but I will be gentler
as we live this life
and find those words

CHEN

when she asked if I ever wanted
to have a child of my own
I remembered Chen

in my imagination,
they always looked like you-
blue eyes, curly black hair,
a nose sprinkled with freckles
and they acted like me-
pouty, bookish, and easily excitable

I could see us reading to them
and trying to figure out when
not to give them what they wanted
exhausted and proud,
after a long day of living
we would fall asleep together
in a toddler-sized bed

      "Maybe."
      I ached

HEARING FROM YOU

hearing from you
was the sound
of the tide coming in
of bass drums
of muteness

I walked sideways all day
stomach warped and sour
like a burnt pancake
in an astronaut's kitchen

my heart beat backwards
taking me away
from the self I knew
the broken horse
the fine-lined hands
the flirtatious smile

as my brain struggled
rubix cube style
with the persistence
of memory

I ADMITTED, YOU SAID

I admitted that
for the first time
in a long time
I didn't know what
I was doing
that maybe I made a mistake
that I was scared and angry

       (Oh, I was angry)

and now I was empty
of all of that
of everything

You said you still loved me
full of the same confidence and fear
you had on the train platform
you said you still wore my flannel
the one I hiked the Grand Canyon in
and the one I hesitated to give to you

You said you still wanted to be together
even though we were all over the map

       "I feel hopeful." I admitted
       "Me too." you said

ACKNOWLEDGMENTS

This book would not have been published without a loving and forceful push from my publisher and best friend, Megan Crayne. Your guidance and dedication have been much needed and much appreciated. Your belief in this book and in me brought something beautiful into an ugly time. Thank you.

To my family, who gave me a last name worth writing about.

To Rissa and Jess for getting me back into writing and reading poetry. Our Dead Poets Society may have been short-lived, but its impact has been long-lasting.

To Kim, for being an honest reader, kind friend, and unflagging emotional support. You see me.

To Katherine, for thinking I was beautiful long before I did. For gifting me with your time, energy, love, and support. You are and will always be my #1 fan. And I'll never forget the meat sweats.

To Anthony, who supported a new me in a new place and became my family.

To Lisa, who covered for me at work whenever I needed to sneak off to write a poem.

To Jess, for supplying me with a tiny Moleskine so I could do the sneaking and the writing.

To the many friends I've made during my wild and wonderful 20s, thank you. Whether it was feedback through texts or keeping quiet on long car rides on the backroads of the Southwest so I could write, you found ways to support my writing and assuage my self-doubts.

To my high school friends and their moms, you were my earliest supporters when I transitioned to writing on Instagram. Your support keeps me going.

To Dr. Lorna Shanks and Wellbutrin XL, for making my life liveable and therefore writable.

To Jay, for showing me that in love I could be content.

Finally, I am especially grateful to you, yes, YOU, for believing in poetry and for picking up this book. You hold in your hands my oldest dream.

Thank you.

ABOUT THE AUTHOR

Taylor L. Ciambra (they/them) is an Italian American nonbinary writer currently living in Portland, Oregon. In 2014, they graduated from Keene State College in Keene, New Hampshire with a degree in Theatre Arts. Currently, they are pursuing a Master's degree in Marriage, Couple, and Family counseling. When they're not writing, hiking, or eating doughnuts, they work to support youth in reaching their behavioral goals.

This is their first published collection of poetry. To see more of their work, visit their website, tlciambra.com or Instagram: @t.l.c.poetry

COLOPHON

This collection is set with the typeface SOLEIL, designed by Wolfgang Homola. The cover font is INTERSTATE, designed by Tobias Frere-Jones.

This collection is printed and distributed through IngramSpark's Lightning Source. Rather than paying for a large-print run, each copy of this collection is printed-on-demand, which reduces waste and helps support a greener, more sustainable publishing industry.

Published by CRAYNE BOOKS, a micro-press operated by a mother-daughter team that publishes new and emerging voices in poetry.

CPSIA information can be obtained
at www.ICGtesting.com
Printed in the USA
JSHW081823021122
32445JS00001B/3